UNDERSTANDING
WEATHER

by Megan Cooley Peterson

PEBBLE
a capstone imprint

Pebble is published by Capstone,
1710 Roe Crest Drive, North Mankato, Minnesota 56003
www.capstonepub.com

Library of Congress Cataloging-in-Publication data is available on the Library of Congress website.
ISBN: 978-1-9771-3352-6 (library binding)
ISBN: 978-1-9771-3346-5 (paperback)
ISBN: 978-1-9771-5519-1 (eBook PDF)

Summary: Explains what weather is, including what causes weather, different types of weather, and the difference between weather and climate.

Editorial Credits
Editor: Mandy Robbins; Designer: Dina Her; Media Researcher: Tracy Cummins; Production Specialist: Katy LaVigne

Photo Credits
iStockphoto: PeopleImages, 16; Science Source: Claus Lunau, 13, Science Stock Photography, 29; Shutterstock: Ami Parikh, 6, andreiuc88, 9, Color4260, design element, djgis, 7, Gregory Johnston, 10, Harvepino, 25, Jakinnboaz, 19, John D Sirlin, 22, Joseph White, 15, Justin Hobson, 23, karelnoppe, 5, Kevin Cass, 4, Kichigin, 20, leonov.o, 12, Mia2you, 24, patpitchaya, 17, Teguh Mujiono, 27, Travelphotoguy, cover, design element, 1, Vitaliy Kaplin, 21

TABLE OF CONTENTS

Words in **bold** are in the glossary.

WHAT IS WEATHER?

Dark clouds fill the sky. Rain drops splat. Lightning flashes. Crack! Thunder booms. Then the clouds move away. The sun shines again.

Weather is what the air and sky are like. It can be hot or cold. It can be rainy or dry. Different places have different weather. Weather can stay the same for a while. It can also change quickly.

People plan for the weather. You get an umbrella when it's raining. During a storm, you stay inside. There, you're safe from strong winds and lightning. Weather helps you decide what to wear too. You wear warm clothing when it is cold. You wear sunglasses when it is sunny.

WEATHER VS. CLIMATE

Weather is not the same as **climate**. Weather can change from day to day. It can even change from minute to minute. Climate is the normal weather patterns in a place over a long period of time. The climate usually stays the same. It has been changing more quickly lately. That is because of **global warming**.

THE SUN

All of Earth's light and heat comes from the sun. The sun's heat makes weather. The ground and water take in the sun's heat. When they let out the heat, the air warms. Air nearest the ground is warmer. Higher in the sky, air is cooler.

The sun doesn't heat Earth evenly. It is warmest near the **equator**. That part of Earth is closest to the sun. It gets the most heat. This uneven heating makes wind.

Wind swirls past the trees.

The sun's heat also helps make clouds. And clouds make rain, snow, and even storms.

TEMPERATURE

Temperature measures how hot or cold the air is. When you go outside, you feel it. You might shiver when it's cold. If it's hot, you sweat.

Temperatures change often. At night, air gets cooler. When the sun rises, air warms. Wind blows cold or warm air into an area. The air is colder in higher places, such as mountains. It is warmest near the equator.

MEASURING TEMPERATURE

A **thermometer** measures temperature. Daniel Gabriel Fahrenheit invented the first thermometer in 1741. It had a glass tube. A bulb at the bottom held a liquid. The liquid heated up. Then it rose up the tube. Marks on the tube showed the temperature. These types of thermometers are still used today.

WIND

Air rises as the sun heats it. Cooler air rushes in below the warmer air. This makes wind. Sometimes, wind has to move over or around an object. Mountains and forests can change the wind's direction. Buildings can change it too.

Jet Streams

Jet streams are bands of strong winds. They are high above Earth. They usually blow from west to east. These winds bend and move north and south. Jet streams move large amounts of air around the world. They cause different kinds of weather.

Jet Streams

Monsoons

A **monsoon** is a wind pattern. It brings warm, wet air to cooler areas. It stretches over a large area. Monsoons are most common in India, Africa, and parts of North America. In summer, these winds bring lots of rain. Farmers need rain to grow crops.

In winter, these winds change directions. Winter monsoons usually bring dry weather. These winds are not as strong as summer winds.

A monsoon in India

RAIN, SNOW, AND STORMS

Rain is water that falls from clouds. Clouds are made from water **droplets**. A cloud forms when **water vapor** in the air rises. This gas cools as it rises. It turns into water droplets. These droplets stick to dust and smoke in the air. They form clouds.

Storm clouds build over a green field.

Sometimes, clouds grow too heavy. The droplets fall to the ground as rain, snow, or hail.

The Water Cycle

All water on Earth goes through a **cycle**. First, the sun warms lakes, oceans, rivers, and streams. Water at the top heats up. It rises into the air as water vapor. This gas forms clouds. Sometimes, the water droplets grow heavier than air. Then they fall back to the ground.

All water is recycled. Rain that fell on the dinosaurs is the same rain that falls today!

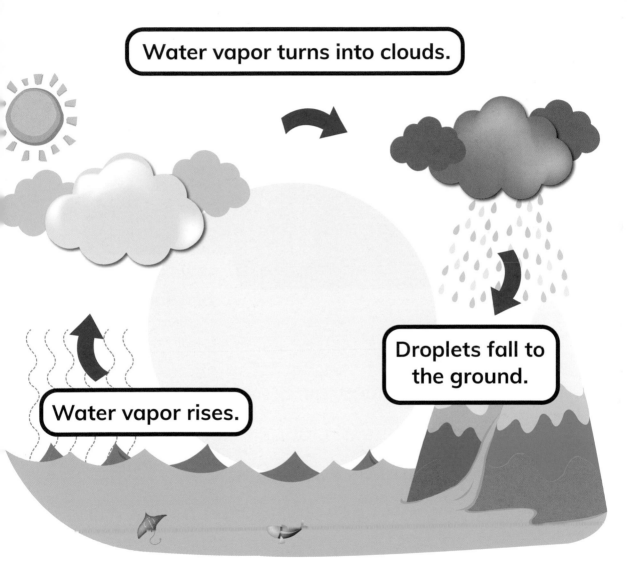

Water vapor turns into clouds.

Droplets fall to the ground.

Water vapor rises.

A close-up view of a snowflake

Snow

In some places, air grows very cold. Water droplets in clouds freeze. They fall to the ground as snow. Snow can fall as **sleet** or snowflakes. Sleet is a mix of rain and snow. A snowflake is a clump of ice crystals. No two snowflakes look alike.

Strong winds and heavy snow can make a blizzard. During a blizzard, it can be hard to see. Winds blow at least 35 miles (56 kilometers) per hour. Snow swirls. Travel is unsafe.

Strong winds blow snow over a road during a blizzard.

Thunderstorms

Lightning flashes. Thunder booms. Thunderstorms usually form in warm, damp weather. They have strong winds and heavy rain. Lightning heats the air around it very fast. The air spreads out quickly. As it snaps back, it makes thunder.

Lightning strikes during a thunderstorm.

Tornadoes

Large thunderstorms can make tornadoes. A tornado is a fast-spinning tube of air. The air can spin as fast as 300 miles (483 km) per hour. Tornadoes rip through buildings and flip cars. People should move to a safe place during a tornado.

A tornado touches down in Colorado.

Hurricanes

Hurricanes are strong storms. They form over warm ocean water. Winds blow up to 200 miles (322 km) per hour. Rain pours. Waves crash into the shore. Hurricanes that move over land can cause flooding. They wreck buildings, homes, bridges, crops, and more.

Hurricane Irma hit Miami Beach, Florida, in 2017.

The center of a hurricane is called the eye. The eye is 10 to 40 miles (16 to 64 km) wide. It is usually calm. A hurricane's wind swirls around it.

This map of a hurricane shows the eye as a dark hole in the center of the swirling clouds.

eye of the hurricane

THE SEASONS

Earth is tilted. It moves around the sun once in a year. When the northern half tilts toward the sun, it is summer there. Days are longer. The air grows warmer. At the same time, the southern half tilts away from the sun. It is winter there. Days are shorter. The air grows cooler.

Earth's tilt doesn't affect **tropical** areas much. They are close to the equator. These places are warm all year. They usually have a rainy and a dry season. Some have rain all year.

Earth's Yearly Rotation Around the Sun

PREDICTING THE WEATHER

Meteorologists study the weather. They use special tools to measure wind speed and rainfall. Tools in space send back pictures of Earth. The pictures show storms and other information. Meteorologists put all this information into super-fast computers. These computers help them **predict** what the weather will do next.

GLOSSARY

climate (KLY-muht)—the average weather of a place throughout the year

cycle (SY-kuhl)—a set of events that happen over and over again

droplet (DRAHP-lit)—a small drop of water

equator (i-KWAY-tuhr)—an imaginary line around the middle of Earth

global warming (GLO-buhl WORM-ing)—a gradual rise in the temperature of the Earth's air

meteorologist (mee-tee-ur-AWL-uh-jist)—a person who studies and predicts the weather

monsoon (mon-SOON)—a very strong seasonal wind that brings heavy rains or hot, dry weather

predict (pri-DIKT)—to say what you think will happen in the future

sleet (SLEET)—rain that freezes as it's falling and hits the ground as frozen pellets of ice

thermometer (thur-MOM-uh-tur)—a tool that measures temperature

tropical (TRAH-pi-kuhl)—near the equator

water vapor (WAH-tur VAY-pur)—water in gas form; water vapor is one of many invisible gases in the air

READ MORE

Hunt, Santana. *The Water Cycle*. New York: Gareth Stevens Publishing, 2020.

Lee, Sally. *Hot Weather: A 4D Book*. North Mankato, MN: Capstone, 2018.

Rotner, Shelley. *What's the Weather?* New York: Holiday House, 2020.

INTERNET SITES

DK Find Out: What Is Weather?
dkfindout.com/us/earth/weather/

Nasa: Climate Kids
climatekids.nasa.gov/menu/weather-and-climate

National Weather Service
weather.gov/owlie/science_kt

INDEX